I could have just
stayed up there
forever.
—SONNY ROLLINS

For all Seekers, like Sonny, who listen
to that *small voice* inside . . . —G.G.

In loving memory of Joan Stevenson,
educator, kid-lit lover, and friend
(Feb. 19, 1937–Dec. 6, 2020) —J.R.

Nancy Paulsen Books
An imprint of Penguin Random House LLC, New York

Text copyright © 2021 by Gary Golio | Illustrations copyright © 2021 by James Ransome
Penguin supports copyright. Copyright fuels creativity, encourages diverse voices, promotes free speech, and
creates a vibrant culture. Thank you for buying an authorized edition of this book and for complying with
copyright laws by not reproducing, scanning, or distributing any part of it in any form without permission.
You are supporting writers and allowing Penguin to continue to publish books for every reader.

Photo of Sonny Rollins by David McLane/*NY Daily News* Archive via Getty Images, used by permission.

Nancy Paulsen Books & colophon are trademarks of Penguin Random House LLC.

Visit us online at penguinrandomhouse.com

Library of Congress Cataloging-in-Publication Data | Names: Golio, Gary, author. | Ransome, James, illustrator. |
Title: Sonny Rollins plays the bridge / Gary Golio; illustrated by James Ransome. | Description: New York:
Nancy Paulsen Books, 2021. | Summary: "Jazz icon Sonny Rollins found an inspired spot to practice his
saxophone when his neighbors complained"—Provided by publisher. | Identifiers: LCCN 2021011562 |
ISBN 9781984813664 (hardcover) | ISBN 9781984813671 (ebook) | ISBN 9781984813688 (ebook) |
Subjects: LCSH: Rollins, Sonny—Juvenile literature. | Jazz musicians—United States—Juvenile literature. |
Saxophonists—United States—Juvenile literature. | Classification: LCC ML3930.R645 G65 2021 |
DDC 788.7/165092 [B]—dc23 | LC record available at https://lccn.loc.gov/2021011562

Manufactured in China by RR Donnelley Asia Printing Solutions Ltd.
ISBN 9781984813664

10 9 8 7 6 5 4 3 2 1

Design by Eileen Savage. Text set in Bommer Slab.
The artwork was done in watercolors and collage.
This is a work of nonfiction. Some names and identifying details have been changed.

SONNY ROLLINS PLAYS THE BRIDGE

written by **GARY GOLIO**

illustrated by **JAMES RANSOME**

Nancy Paulsen Books

the Bridge

leaps
spreads its wings
joyfully
joining shore to shore

steel towers
standing tall
reaching high
touching
sky

lifting
trains cars people
floating all
here to there
through the air

&
the River
stretched out below
a shiny
endless
song

the City
has spaces
large and small
room
for
all

but

when you can't
play in your apartment
(shhh—the neighbors!)
you can
play outside
if
you know where

So Sonny
walks down Delancey

comes from home
carrying his case
moving through space

ahead
is that a
strange
place
to play his
horn

or is it
strange
to listen to
that
small voice
inside
which says

you need to do this

even if
everyone
wonders
WHY
?

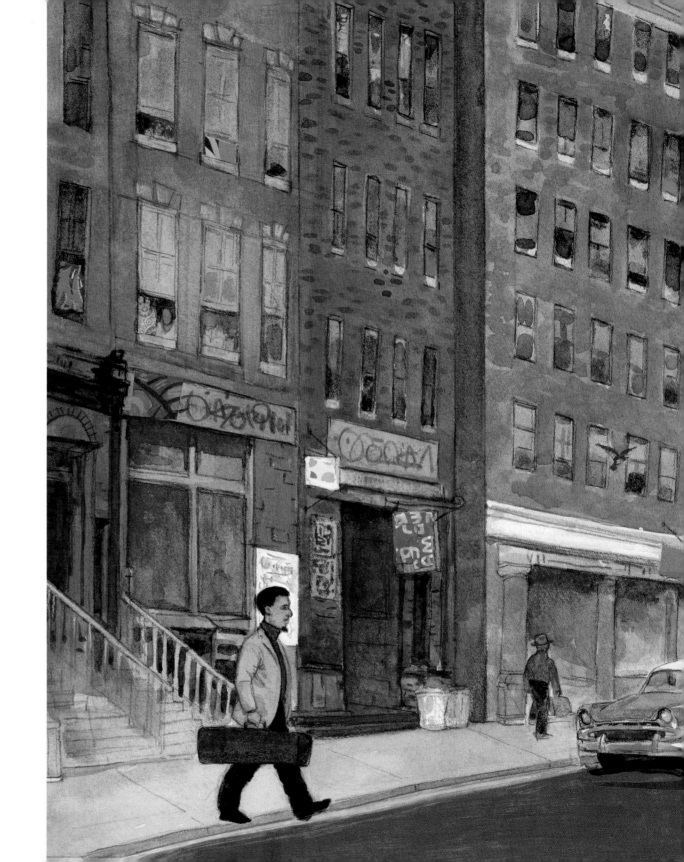

Sonny
climbs the steps to the Bridge
to the walkway at the top
&
strolls above
the sprawling
spider city
with
millions of lives
lights
movement and speed
lots of
sound
&
lots of
noise

the Bridge
=
a place to
play
a place
to be alone
with just
YOU

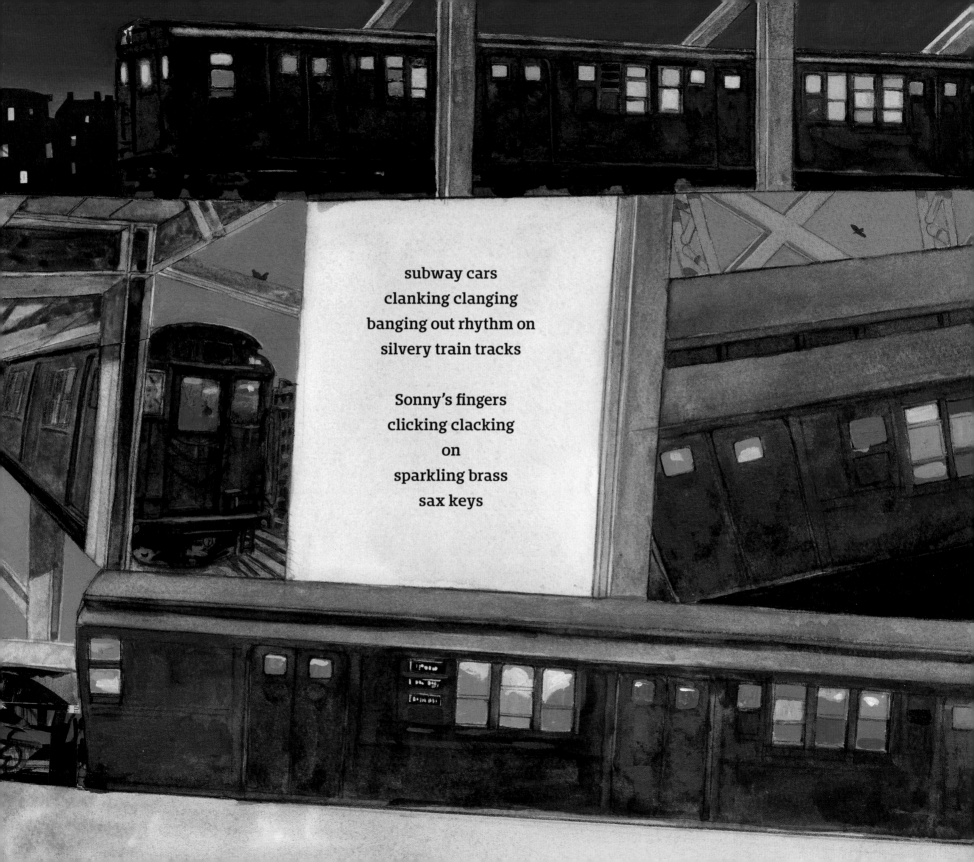

subway cars
clanking clanging
banging out rhythm on
silvery train tracks

Sonny's fingers
clicking clacking
on
sparkling brass
sax keys

tugboats
blowing bass notes
back
and forth

Sonny answering
note-for-note
with
low moans
of his
own

&

high-pitched
seagull cries
echoing
Sonny's funny
squeaks
&
squawks

a giant
Bridge
that
strides the
River

a giant
jazzman
who
strides the
Bridge

here
Sonny
can play
anything

EVERYTHING

that
comes into his
mind

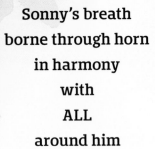

Sonny's breath
borne through horn
in harmony
with
ALL
around him

above
the sky
deep and blue
spread out
like a
smile
over Earth

below
Sonny's mind
open wide
spread out
like a net
catching
what falls
&
drawing notes
down
down
down from the
sky

*

and again

the Bridge
leaps
spreads its wings
just like
Sonny

Sonny on the Bridge

WHO IS SONNY ROLLINS?

In 1959, when Sonny Rollins was just twenty-nine years old, he walked away from a *big* career—playing music with famous people in famous places—because he didn't think he was *as good as they said*. For two years, supported by his wife, Sonny went up to the pedestrian walkway atop the Williamsburg Bridge and blew his horn. Alone. To the sky, the trains, the tugboats and the East River. He was practicing in the open air to get better. To *be* better. Not just as a musician, but as a human being. Because that's who Sonny Rollins is.

They call him the Colossus for a reason. Not only because of his size (he stands well over six feet), but out of respect for someone whose energy, knowledge, and experience make him a force of nature. Now ninety, Sonny's still a jazz giant, one of the few left from the Golden Age of Jazz, who's played with all the greats, including John Coltrane, Thelonius Monk, Miles Davis, Charlie Parker, Dizzy Gillespie, and Ornette Coleman.

Theodore Walter "Sonny" Rollins was just a boy when he caught the music bug in Harlem, where he grew up. It was a place overflowing with culture and creativity. And his heroes were all around him—walking down the street, playing in local clubs, even sitting in the movie theater. Inspired by horn players like Coleman Hawkins and Louis Jordan, Sonny got his first saxophone at age nine and played in his clothes closet so he wouldn't bother the neighbors. Practicing for hours at a time just seemed natural, and he was working in bands even before graduating high school. Money,

SONNY ROLLINS ON THE WILLIAMSBURG BRIDGE, JUNE 1966

fame, and all sorts of temptations followed. It was a lot to handle—the kind of thing that can make you lose your way unless you learn to stay strong.

So when Sonny walked away from the music scene and went up to the Williamsburg Bridge, he surprised a lot of people. They didn't understand that Sonny knew exactly what he was doing—listening to the small voice inside that said to put himself, and his *music*, before everything else.

It takes courage to make choices like that. But that's who Sonny Rollins is.

THE BRIDGE

The Williamsburg Bridge took a lot of grief for a very long time. Famous for being the longest suspension bridge in the world when it was finished in 1903, it was also considered the *ugliest* by many New Yorkers in love with its older neighbor, the Brooklyn Bridge.

Today, because of its renovated upper walkways and bike lanes, the Williamsburg Bridge is beloved by young and old. It's a real workhorse—carrying more than 130,000 people each day between Brooklyn and Manhattan by car, subway train, bicycle, and on foot—and has been featured in many books (*A Tree Grows in Brooklyn, The Last Olympian*) and movies (*The Dark Knight Rises, The Amazing Spider-Man*). It's also the place where jazz saxophonist Sonny Rollins went in 1959 to play his horn out in the open air, above the river and under the sky. There's even a movement underway to rename the bridge in his honor!

In 1961, Sonny returned to the music scene, and in 1962 he recorded a series of songs called simply *The Bridge*. It's probably his most beloved album and perhaps, more than any-thing else, Sonny's way of saying *thank you* to his old friend.

SONNY'S WORDS

This book grew out of many conversations with Sonny Rollins speaking about his experiences on planet Earth. Playing music has taken him all over the world, but these days he lives a pretty quiet life. How does he spend his time? "I try to do good work and be a good person—that's all up to me. I believe in the Great Spirit, and trying to learn something new each day." After more than ninety years, what does Sonny think is important? "There's only one truth—the Golden Rule—to treat people the way you want to be treated. You've got to be good, to be kind, and not hurt anyone. And you gotta give, give, give." About his time on the Williamsburg Bridge, he speaks very simply: "You have to know yourself. To listen to that small voice inside. Never mind what people say. Do you know what you want? Do you know who you are? Do you know who the person in the mirror is? That's what it's all about. The rest doesn't mean diddly!"

Sonny's official website is SonnyRollins.com, and you can both watch him play and listen to his music on sites like YouTube. Some songs to look for include "The Bridge," "St. Thomas," "I'm an Old Cowhand," and "God Bless the Child."